Vegan Pressure Cooker Cookbook

50+ Healthy Recipes that you Can Make in Half the Time to Live a Healthier Life and Lose Weight

July Kern

Table Of Contents

Introduction

Nowadays veganism is one of the most popular trends all over the world. Thousands of people prefer to refuse animal products and follow a natural lifestyle. A vegan diet has started its history since the 1944 year and in five years later Leslie J Cross suggested to get the definition for veganism. He supported the idea of the emancipation of animals from the human's exploitation. During the years the definition of veganism had been modified and now it became the lifestyle which supports respectful attitude to animals and nature in general.

Veganism is the type of vegetarianism which implies the restriction of meat, poultry, seafood, and dairy products. What do vegans eat? The vegan diet is very diverse. There are a million recipes that can satisfy the most demanded tastes. Cakes, pastries, pies, stews, curries – each of this meal is included in a vegan diet. There is only one condition: every meal should be cooked from plant-based ingredients. Vegans get all the vital vitamins, minerals, and proteins from vegetables, fruits, grains, nuts, and seeds.

Breakfast

1. Morning Muffins

Prep: 10 minutes **Cooking:** 10 minutes**Servings:** 5

Ingredients:

- 1 banana, chopped 1 teaspoon vanilla extract

- 1 tablespoon cocoa powder

- 4 tablespoon flax meal 4 teaspoon almond butter 3 teaspoon white sugar

- 2 tablespoons almond milk

- ½ teaspoon baking powder

- 1 cup water, for cooking

Directions:

1. Blend chopped banana until smooth and transfer it in the mixingbowl.

2. Add vanilla extract, cocoa powder, flax

meal, almond butter, white sugar, almond milk, and baking powder.

3. Mix up the mixture and place it in the muffin molds. Fill ½ part of every muffin mold.

4. Pour water in the instant pot and set the rack.

5. Place the muffins on the rack and close the lid.

6. Cook the muffins for 10 minutes on Manual mode (High pressure). After this, make quick pressure release.

7. Chill the muffins for 3-4 minutes before serving.

Nutrition value/serving: calories 152, fat 10.9, fiber 4, carbs 13.1, protein 4.5

2. Soy Yogurt

Prep time: 10 minutes **Cooking time:** 11 hours

Servings: 6

Ingredients:

- 2 cups of soy milk

- 2 probiotic capsules

- 1 cup strawberries, chopped

Directions:

1. Pour 1 ½ cup of soy milk in the big jar.

2. Mix up together remaining soy milk with probiotic capsules andwhisk well.

3. Then mi up together all soy milk and stir.

4. After this, pour it in the yogurt jars and insert in the instant pot.

5. Set the "Yogurt" mode and close the lid.

6. Cook yogurt for 11 hours.

7. When the time is over – place the yogurt in the fridge to chill and to start the process of probiotic development.

8. Add strawberries directly before serving.

Nutrition value/serving: calories 52, fat 1.5, fiber 1, carbs 7, protein 2.8

3. Coconut Yogurt with Berries

Prep time: 10 minutes **Cooking time:** 4 hours

Servings: 4

Ingredients:

- ¾ cup blueberries

- ¾ cup blackberries

- 1 teaspoon chia seeds

- 1 cup of coconut milk

- 1 tablespoon coconut yogurt

- 2 tablespoons white sugar

Directions:

1. Pour coconut milk in the instant pot bowl.

2. Set yogurt mode and adjust the setting to get "to boil".

3. Cook the coconut milk until it reaches

100F. Use the cookingthermometer for this step.

4. Then add coconut yogurt and stir it until homogenous.

5. Close the lid and leave on the yogurt mode for 3-4 hours.

6. When the time is over – you will get a thick creamy mixture.

7. Transfer it on the cheesecloth and squeeze gently.

8. Then place the yogurt in the yogurt jars.

9. Before serving add chia seeds, blackberries, and blueberries.

Nutrition value/serving: calories 198, fat 15.1, fiber 4, carbs 16.8, protein 2.3

4. Breakfast Potatoes

Prep time: 10 minutes **Cooking time:** 21 minutes

Servings: 4

Ingredients:

- 4 potatoes, peeled

- 1 tablespoon coconut oil

- ½ teaspoon dried cilantro

- 1 teaspoon salt

- ½ teaspoon ground black pepper

- 1 teaspoon dried parsley

- 1 teaspoon dried dill

- ¼ cup of water 1 red pepper, chopped

- 1 white onion, chopped

Directions:

1. Chop potatoes and place in the instant pot.

2. Add coconut oil, dried cilantro, salt, ground black pepper, driedparsley, and dill.

3. Stir the ingredients, set Saute mode and cook it for 6 minutes.Stir time to time.

4. Then add red pepper and white onion. Stir.

5. Add water and close the lid.

6. Set the Manual mode (Low pressure) and cook potatoes for 15minutes or until the potatoes are tender.

Nutrition value/serving: calories 198, fat 3.7, fiber 6.2, carbs 38.6, protein

4.3

5. Rice with Maple Syrup

Prep time: 8 minutes **Cooking time:** 15 minutes

Servings: 5

Ingredients:

- 1 cup of rice

- 2 cups almond milk

- 1 teaspoon vanilla extract

- ¼ cup maple syrup

- 1 teaspoon almond butter

Directions:

1. Place rice in the instant pot.

2. Add almond milk and vanilla extract. Stir gently and close the lid.

3. Set the "Rice" mode and cook rice for 15

minutes.

4. Then add almond butter and maple syrup. Stir it.

Nutrition value/serving: calories 419, fat 25, fiber 2.9, carbs 46.2, protein

5.5

Burgers and Patties

6. Lentil Burger

Pep: 20 minutes **Cooking:** 26 minutes**Servings:** 7

Ingredients:

- 1 cup lentils, soaked overnight

- 1 cup of water ½ carrot, peeled

- 1 teaspoon cayenne pepper

- 4 tablespoon wheat flour 1 teaspoon salt

- 1 teaspoon olive oil 1 tablespoon dried dill

Directions:

1. Put lentils to the Instant pot together with water, carrot, salt, andcayenne pepper.

2. Close the lid and set Manual mode (High pressure).

3. Cook the ingredients for 25 minutes and allow natural pressurerelease for 10 minutes.

4. Transfer the cooked ingredients in the blender and blend untilsmooth.

5. Add wheat flour and dried dill. Mix it up until smooth. If the mixture is liquid – add more flour.

6. Make the burgers and place them together with the olive oil inthe instant pot.

7. Set Manual mode (High pressure) for 1 minutes (quick pressurerelease).

8. It is recommended to serve burgers warm.

Nutrition value/serving: calories 122, fat 1.1, fiber 8.7, carbs 20.7, protein 7.7

7. Black Beans Burger

Prep time: 15 minutes **Cooking time:** 5 minutes

Servings: 5

Ingredients:

- 1 cup black beans, cooked

- 2 tablespoon bread crumbs

- 1 teaspoon salt

- ¼ cup sweet corn, cooked

- 1 teaspoon turmeric

- 1 tablespoon fresh parsley, chopped

- ½ yellow sweet pepper, chopped

- ½ cup of water

Directions:

1. Mash the black beans until you get puree and combine together with salt, sweet corn,

turmeric, parsley, and sweet pepper.

2. Mix it up carefully with the help of a
   spoon.

3. Add bread crumbs and stir again.

4. Pour water in the instant pot bowl and
   insert steamer rack.

5. Make the burgers from the black bean
mixture and freeze themfor 30 minutes.

6. Then wrap every burger in the foil and
place on the steamerrack.

7. Close the lid and cook on Manual mode
(High pressure) for 5minutes.

8. Then allow natural pressure release for 5
   minutes.

9. Remove the foil from the burgers and

transfer on the plate.Garnish burgers with lettuce leaves if desired.

Nutrition value/serving: calories 155, fat 0.9, fiber 6.5, carbs 28.8, protein 9.2

8. Mushroom Burger

Prep time: 10 minutes **Cooking time:** 14 minutes

Servings: 4

Ingredients:

- 2 cups mushrooms, chopped

- 1 onion, diced

- ½ cup silken tofu

- ½ teaspoon salt

- ½ teaspoon chili flakes

- 1 tablespoon dried parsley

- 1 teaspoon dried dill

- 3 tablespoon flax meal

- ½ teaspoon olive oil

Directions:

1. Put mushrooms in the blender and grind.

2. Then transfer the vegetables to the instant pot together withonion, and olive oil.

3. Stir gently and close the lid. Cook ingredients on Saute mode for10 minutes.

4. Meanwhile, mash silken tofu until you get a puree. Mix it up with salt, chili flakes, dried parsley, and dried dill. Add flax meal and pulse for 10 seconds.

5. When the mushroom mixture is cooked transfer it in the bowl and combines together with the silken tofu.

6. Stir well.

7. Make the burgers.

8. Line the instant pot pan with baking paper and place burgers on

it.

9. Close the lid and meal for 4 minutes on

High. Then use quick

pressure release.

10. Chill the burgers till the room

temperature beforeserving.

Nutrition value/serving: calories 47, fat 2.6, fiber

2.5, carbs 5.4, protein

2.6

9. Seitan Burger

Prep time: 10 minutes **Cooking time:** 2 minutes

Servings: 1

Ingredients:

- 1 burger bun
- 1 teaspoon mustard
- 1 teaspoon soy sauce
- 1 seitan steak
- 1 teaspoon onion powder
- 1 teaspoon olive oil
- 1 tablespoon apple cider vinegar

Directions:

1. Make sauce for seitan steak: mix up together soy sauce, onion powder, olive oil, and apple cider vinegar.

2. Brush seitan steak with sauce from each side and place in theinstant pot.

3. Close the lid and cook on Manual mode (High pressure) for 2 minutes (quick pressure release).

4. Meanwhile, cut burger bun into halves and spread with mustard.

5. Place seitan steak on the one half of burger bun and cover withthe second one.

Nutrition value/serving: calories 303, fat 8.8, fiber 2.8, carbs 24.9, protein 26.8

10.   Spinach Patties

Prep time: 10 minutes **Cooking time:** 10 minutes

Servings: 7

Ingredients:

- 3 cups spinach, chopped

- 2 tablespoon coconut shred

- 4 tablespoon panko bread crumbs

- 1 teaspoon salt ½ teaspoon chili flakes

- 2 tablespoon flax meal

- 6 tablespoon hot water

- 1 teaspoon olive oil

- 1 tablespoon coconut yogurt

Directions:

1. In the mixing bowl mix up together flax meal and hot water. Whisk the mixture.

2. Then add coconut shred, panko bread crumbs, spinach, chili flakes, coconut yogurt, and salt.

3. Mix up the mixture until homogenous.

4. Set the Saute mode in Instant pot and preheat it until shows"Hot".

5. Then brush instant bowl with olive oil from inside.

6. Make patties from the spinach mixture with the help of 2 spoons and place them in the instant pot.

7. Saute them for 10 minutes. You can flip the patties duringcooking if desired.

Nutrition value/serving: calories 47, fat 2.9, fiber 1.3, carbs 4.5, protein 1.5

Side Dishes

11. Mashed Potato

Pre time: 10 minutes **Cooking time:** 10 minutes

Servings: 6

Ingredients:

- 6 potatoes, peeled, chopped

- 1 cup of water

- ¼ cup of coconut milk

- 1 tablespoon coconut yogurt

- 1 teaspoon salt

- 1 tablespoon chives, chopped

Directions:

1. Place potato and water in the instant pot.

   Add salt and close the

lid.

2. Cook the vegetables on Manual mode for 10 minutes.

3. Then use quick pressure release.

4. Open the lid, drain water from the potatoes and mash them.

5. Add coconut yogurt, coconut milk, and chopped chives.

6. Mix it up until soft and smooth.

Nutrition value/serving: calories 171, fat 2.6, fiber 5.3, carbs 34.2, protein 3.9

12.   Vermicelli Bowl

Prep time: 10 minutes **Cooking time:** 6 minutes

Servings: 2

Ingredients:

- 1 cup vermicelli, roasted

- ½ yellow onion, diced

- ½ jalapeno pepper, chopped

- 1 cup of water

- 1 teaspoon ground cumin

- ¼ teaspoon ground coriander

- 1 teaspoon dried rosemary

- 1 teaspoon ground ginger

- 2 red bell peppers, chopped 1 teaspoon olive oil

Directions:

1. Put diced onion, jalapeno pepper, ground

cumin, coriander, rosemary, ginger, and bell peppers in the instant pot.

2. Add olive oil, stir it and saute for 3 minutes.

3. Then add vermicelli and water. Close the lid and set manual mode (High pressure) for 3 minutes.

4. Make a quick pressure release.

5. Shake the meal with the help of fork gently and transfer into thebowls.

Nutrition value/serving: calories 184, fat 3.6, fiber 3.8, carbs 34.3, protein 5.3

13.   Broccoli Rice

Prep time: 10 minutes **Cooking time:** 1 minute

Servings: 4

Ingredients:

- 2 ½ cup broccoli florets

- 1 teaspoon salt

- 1 teaspoon grinded peppercorn

- ½ cup of water

- 1 teaspoon olive oil

- 1 teaspoon minced garlic

Directions:

1. Put broccoli florets in the food processor and blend until you getbroccoli rice.

2. Pour water in the instant pot.

3. Then place broccoli rice in the instant pot

pan.

4. Add peppercorns, salt, olive oil, and minced garlic. Mix up theingredients.

5. Transfer the pan in the instant pot and close the lid.

6. Set manual mode and cook on High for 1 minute. Make a quickpressure release.

7. Chill the cauliflower rice for 2-5 minutes before serving.

Nutrition value/serving: calories 32, fat 1.4, fiber 1.6, carbs 4.4, protein

1.7

14.　Sweet Potato Mash

Prep time: 10 minutes **Cooking time:** 9 minutes

Servings: 6

Ingredients:

- 2 cups sweet potatoes, peeled, chopped

- 1 teaspoon salt

- 1 teaspoon ground black pepper

- 1 cup vegetable broth

- 1 tablespoon fresh parsley, chopped

Directions:

1. Put potatoes, salt, and vegetable broth in the instant pot.

2. Close the lid and set manual mode. Cook on High for 9 minutes.

3. Then make quick pressure release, strain

the sweet potatoes andmash until smooth.

4. Add chopped parsley and ground black pepper in the mashedsweet potato. Mix up well.

Nutrition value/serving: calories 67, fat 0.3, fiber 2.2, carbs 14.4, protein

1.6

15.   Red Cabbage with Apples

Prep time: 10 minutes **Cooking time:** 7 minutes

Servings: 3

Ingredients:

- 1-pound red cabbage

- 1 apple, chopped

- 1 teaspoon salt

- ¼ cup of coconut milk

- ¾ cup almond milk

- ½ teaspoon chili flakes

Directions:

1. Shred red cabbage and mix it up with salt.

2. Transfer the mixture in the instant pot. Add coconut milk,almond milk, and chili flakes.

3. Then add apple and set manual mode

(High pressure).

4. Cook the cabbage for 7 minutes. Then allow natural pressurerelease.

5. Transfer the meal into the serving bowls and mix up well beforeserving.

Nutrition value/serving: calories 123, fat 5.1, fiber 6, carbs 20.2, protein 2.6

Grains and Pasta

16.   Vanilla Rice Pudding

Prep: 10 minutes **Cooking:** 14 minutes**Servings:** 4

Ingredients:

- 1 cup of rice ● 1 teaspoon cornstarch

- 2 teaspoon vanilla extract

- 1 cup almond milk ● ½ cup of water

- 1 cup of coconut milk

- 4 tablespoons maple syrup

- ¼ teaspoon ground nutmeg

- ½ teaspoon ground cardamom

- 4 teaspoon raisins

Directions:

9. Whisk together cornstarch, water, vanilla

extract, almond milk, coconut milk, ground nutmeg, and ground cardamom.

10.   Place rice in the instant pot bowl, add liquid mixture,and mix it up.

11.   Close and seal the lid and set Rice mode. Set timer for 4minutes (High pressure).

12.   Then allow natural pressure release for 10 minutes.

13.   Open the lid and mix up pudding.

14.   Transfer it into the bowls and sprinkle with raisins andmaple syrup.

Nutrition value/serving: calories 393, fat 15.4, fiber 2.1, carbs 59.2,

protein 5.1

17.　Oatmeal with Tender Onions

Prep time: 15 minutes **Cooking time:** 5 minutes

Servings: 5

Ingredients:

- 2 cups cut oats

- 1 red onion, sliced

- 1 tablespoon coconut oil

- ½ teaspoon salt

- 2 cups of water

- ½ teaspoon white pepper

Directions:

10.　　　Preheat instant pot on Saute mode and toss coconut oilinside.

11.　　　Melt it and add onions, salt, and white pepper. Mix it upand saute for 2 minutes.

12.   Then add cut oats and water.

13.   Close and seal the lid and set Manual mode (highpressure).

14.   Cook oatmeal for 3 minutes. Then allow natural pressure release for 15 minutes more.

15.   Mix up the cooked meal well before serving.

Nutrition value/serving: calories 99, fat 4.2, fiber 2.1, carbs 13.4, protein 2.6

18.   Cayenne Pepper Corn

Prep time: 5 minutes **Cooking time:** 4 minutes

Servings: 4

Ingredients:

- 2 cups corn, frozen

- 1 teaspoon cayenne pepper

- 1 teaspoon fresh parsley, chopped

- ½ cup vegetable broth

- 1 teaspoon olive oil

- ½ teaspoon salt

Directions:

11.   Place corn and vegetable broth in the instant pot bowl.

12.   Sprinkle the ingredients with parsley, cayenne pepper,salt, and olive oil.

13.   Stir the mixture gently with the
help of the spatula,close and seal the lid.

14.   Cook the corn on Manual mode
(high pressure) for 4minutes.

15.   Then use quick pressure release.

Nutrition value/serving: calories 82, fat 2.3, fiber
2.2, carbs 14.9, protein
3.2

19.   PopCorn

Prep: 2 minutes **Cooking:** 10 minutes**Servings:** 2

Ingredients:

- ½ cup of corn ● 1 teaspoon olive oil

- 1 teaspoon salt

Drections:

6. Set Saute mode and pour olive oil in the instant pot.

7. Preheat it and add corn.

8. Sprinkle corn with salt and stir carefully.

9. Close the lid and cook popcorn on Saute mode for 7-10 minutesor until it is cooked.

Nutrition value/serving: calories 53, fat 2.8, fiber 1.1, carbs 7.3, protein 1.3

20.   Teff in Tomato Paste

Prep time: 10 minutes **Cooking time:** 6 minutes

Servings: 3

Ingredients:

- 1 cup teff

- 2 cups vegetable broth

- 1 teaspoon salt

- 1 teaspoon tomato paste

- 1 teaspoon coconut oil

Directions:

8. Toss coconut oil in the instant pot bowl.

9. Set Saute mode and preheat coconut oil until it is melted.

10.   Add tomato paste and salt. Stir gently.

11.   After this, add teff and stir well. Saute it for 3 minutes.

12.   Add vegetable broth, close and seal the lid.

13.   Cook the meal on Manual mode (High pressure) for 3minutes.

14.   Then use quick pressure release.

15.   Mix up the meal before serving.

Nutrition value/serving: calories 255, fat 3.2, fiber 8.1, carbs 45, protein 11.3

Beans and Lentils

21. Lentil Tacos

Prep time: 10 minutes **Cooking time:** 10 minutes

Servings: 6

Ingredients:

- 1 cup lentils

- 1 teaspoon salt

- 1 cup vegetable broth

- 2 cups salsa

- 1 teaspoon garlic powder

- ½ teaspoon onion powder

- 6 tablespoons coconut yogurt ● 6 corn tortillas

Directions:

7. Place lentil, salt, salsa, and vegetable

broth in the instant potbowl.

8. Add garlic powder and onion powder. Close the lid.

9. Cook the lentils on Manual for 10 minutes. Then make quickpressure release.

10.   When the lentils are cooked, open the lid and chill them at least till the room temperature.

11.   Fill corn tortillas with the lentils mixture and sprinklewith coconut yogurt.

Nutrition value/serving: calories 200, fat 1.4, fiber 12.9, carbs 37.2,

protein 11.3

22.   Red Kidney Beans Burrito

Prep time: 10 minutes **Cooking time:** 15 minutes

Servings: 2

Ingredients:

- ½ avocado, sliced

- 1 bell pepper, sliced

- ½ onion, peeled

- 1 tablespoon olive oil

- 1 teaspoon tomato paste

- ½ teaspoon chili flakes

- ½ cup red kidney beans, canned

- ½ teaspoon ground cumin

- ½ teaspoon ground coriander

- ½ cup fresh cilantro, chopped

- 2 burritos

Directions:

6. Preheat instant pot on Saute mode for 3 minutes.

7. Pour olive oil and add sliced bell pepper. Start to sautevegetable, stir it from time to time.

8. Meanwhile cut the onion into the petals and add in the instantpot too.

9. Add chili flakes, ground cumin, coriander, and tomato paste. Stir it and add red kidney beans. Mix it up.

10. Close the lid and saute the mixture for 10 minutes.

11. Then switch off the instant pot and open the lid.

12. Fill the burritos with the bean mixture, add

cilantro, avocado, androll.

Nutrition value/serving: calories 352, fat 17.6, fiber

11.9, carbs 40.3,

protein 12.4

23.   Lentil Meatballs

Prep time: 10 minutes **Cooking time:** 20 minute

Servings: 4

Ingredients:

- 1 ½ cup lentils

- 3 cups of water

- 1 teaspoon salt

- 1 tablespoon olive oil

- 1 teaspoon turmeric

- 1 teaspoon dried oregano

- 1 teaspoon dried dill • 1 carrot, grated

- 2 tablespoons oatmeal flour

- 1 onion, diced

Directions:

8. Pour water in the instant pot.

9. Add lentils and salt and close the lid. Cook it on Manual mode for 7 minutes. Then use quick pressure release.

10. Meanwhile, mix up together grated carrot and diced onion.

11. Transfer the cooked lentils in the mixing bowl.

12. Pour olive oil in the instant pot and add carrot mixture.

13. Close the lid and saute it for 10 minutes. Open the lid and stir it from time to time.

14. When the carrot mixture is cooked, transfer it in the lentils.

15. Add turmeric, dried oregano, and

dill. Then add oatmeal flour and mix up until smooth and homogenous.

16.   Make the medium size meatballs from the lentil mixture and transfer in the instant pot.

17.   Set Saute mode, close the lid and cook the meal for 3 minutes.

Nutrition value/serving: calories 313, fat 4.5, fiber 23.5, carbs 49.4,

protein 19.5

24.   Black Beans Chili

Prep time: 10 minutes **Cooking time:** 15 minutes

Servings: 4

Ingredients:

- 1 cup black beans, canned

- 1 cup vegetable broth

- 1 cup tomato sauce

- 1 cup fresh cilantro, chopped

- 1 teaspoon chili flakes

- 1 teaspoon ground coriander

- 1 teaspoon dried rosemary

- 1 chipotle pepper, chopped

- 2 sweet green pepper, chopped

- 1 garlic clove, diced

- 3 tomatoes, chopped

- 1 red onion, roughly chopped

- 1 tablespoon almond butter

- 1 teaspoon garlic powder

Directions:

5. Melt the almond butter in the instant pot on Saute mode.

6. Add diced garlic onion, garlic powder, green pepper, chipotle,rosemary, coriander, chili flakes, vegetable broth, and stir well.

7. Saute the ingredients for 10 minutes.

8. After this, add black beans and tomato sauce. Mix up the chilivery carefully.

9. Add tomatoes, close and seal the lid.

10.   Set Manual mode and cook chili for 3 minutes, usequick pressure release.

11.   Open the lid and mix up chili well.

12.   Transfer the cooked meal in the serving bowls and sprinkle with chopped cilantro.

Nutrition value/serving: calories 264, fat 3.8, fiber 11.9, carbs 45.6,

protein 15.5

25.   Burrito Bowl

Prep time: 10 minutes **Cooking time:** 7 minutes

Servings: 2

Ingredients:

- 1 cup of water

- 1 cup quinoa

- 1 teaspoon salt

- 1 teaspoon ground cumin

- ½ cup red beans, cooked

- 1 bell pepper, chopped

- ½ avocado, sliced

- ¼ cup of coconut milk

Directions:

6. Transfer quinoa and water in the instant pot. Add salt, bellpepper, and close the lid.

7. Seal and set Manual mode.

8. Cook the ingredients for 7 minutes. Then use quick pressurerelease.

9. Transfer the cooked quinoa mixture in the bowl. Add red beansand ground cumin. Mix up well.

10. Add avocado slices and sprinkle the meal with thecoconut milk.

Nutrition value/serving: calories 662, fat 23, fiber 17.9, carbs 93.7, protein

24.8

Soup and Stews

26.   Potato Chowder with Corn

Prep time: 10 minutes **Cooking time:** 10 minutes

Servings: 2

Ingredients:

- ¼ cup mushrooms, chopped

- ½ onion, diced

- 1 cup coconut cream

- 1 cup of water

- ½ cup corn kernels

- 1 teaspoon salt

- 1 teaspoon paprika

- ½ teaspoon chili flakes

- 1 cup potato, chopped

- 1 teaspoon olive oil

Directions:

16.   In the instant pot mix up together diced onion and mushrooms. Add olive oil and saute vegetables for 3-4 minutes or until golden brown.

17.   Then transfer vegetables in the bowl.

18.   Add water and coconut cream in the instant pot.

19.   Then add potato and corn kernels. Sprinkle the mixture with salt, paprika, and chili flakes.

20.   Set Manual mode (High pressure), close and seal the

lid.

21.   Cook chowder for 5 minutes. Then allow natural pressure release for 5 minutes.

22.   Ladle the cooked chowder in the bowls and sprinkle with cooked onion and mushrooms.

Nutrition value/serving: calories 374, fat 31.6, fiber 5.6, carbs 23.9, protein 5.5

27. Leek Soup

Prep time: 10 minutes **Cooking time:** 35 minutes

Servings: 4

Ingredients:

- 3 cups leek, chopped

- 2 tablespoons coconut oil

- 1 teaspoon minced garlic

- 1 cup potatoes, chopped

- 1 tablespoon corn flour

- ½ cup coconut cream

- 3 cups of water

- ½ cup celery root, chopped

- 1 teaspoon salt

- 1 teaspoon chili flakes

- ½ teaspoon ground ginger

- ½ teaspoon white pepper

- 4 teaspoons chives, chopped

Directions:

16.   Place leek with coconut oil in the instant pot.

17.   Add minced garlic, and saute the mixture for 5 minutes. Stir it from time to time.

18.   When the vegetables are soft, sprinkle them with cornflour.

19.   Add chopped celery root, potatoes, coconut cream, water, chili flakes, ground ginger, and white pepper.

20.   Mix it up and close the lid.

21.   Set Saute mode and cook soup for 30 minutes.

22.   Then blend the soup until you get a creamy mixture.

23.   Garnish the cooked soup with chopped chives.

Nutrition value/serving: calories 212, fat 14.4, fiber 3.4, carbs 20.8,

protein 2.9

28. French Onion Soup

Prep time: 10 minutes **Cooking time:** 25 minutes

Servings: 2

Ingredients:

- 3 cups onion, diced

- 2 tablespoons coconut oil

- ¼ cup of water

- 2 cups vegetable broth

- 1 teaspoon salt

- 1 teaspoon ground black pepper

- 1 teaspoon minced garlic

- ½ teaspoon ground nutmeg

- 3 oz vegan Parmesan, grated

Directions:

13.   Place diced onions and coconut

oil in the instant pot.

14.	Set saute mode and start to cook them.

15.	Sprinkle the vegetables with salt, ground black pepper, minced garlic, and ground nutmeg. Stir well.

16.	When the onions start to become tender, add water and mix up the mixture well.

17.	Close and seal the lid.

18.	Set Manual mode (High pressure) and cook onions for 12 minutes. Then use quick pressure release.

19.	Add vegetable broth and stir the soup well. Close the lid and cook on Saute mode for 10 minutes more.

20.   Mix up the soup carefully and ladle into the servingbowls.

21.   Top the cooked onion soup with vegan Parmesan.

Nutrition value/serving: calories 332, fat 14, fiber 4.6, carbs 27.7, protein

19.5

29.   Potato Cream Soup

Prep time: 5 minutes **Cooking time:** 15 minutes

Servings: 4

Ingredients:

- 1 cup of coconut milk

- 2 cups of water

- 2 cups potatoes, chopped

- 1 onion, sliced

- 1 teaspoon turmeric

- 1 teaspoon salt

- 1 tablespoon avocado oil

- 1 teaspoon chili flakes

- ½ cup fresh cilantro, chopped

Directions:

13.   Pour avocado oil in the instant

pot and preheat it onSaute mode.

14.   When the oil is hot, add sliced onion and choppedpotatoes.

15.   Sprinkle the vegetables with turmeric, salt, and chili flakes. Mix up the ingredients and saute for 5 minutes.

16.   Then add coconut milk and water. Close and seal the

lid.

17.   Cook soup on Manual mode for 10 minutes. Then use

quick pressure release.

18.   Open the lid and blend soup with the help of the handblender.

19.   When the liquid is smooth,

transfer it into the servingbowls.

20.   Sprinkle the soup with cilantro

before serving.

Nutrition value/serving: calories 208, fat 14.9, fiber

4.1, carbs 18.3,

protein 3.1

30.   Quinoa Tomato Soup

Prep time: 5 minutes **Cooking time:** 15 minutes

Servings: 3

Ingredients:

- 1 carrot, diced ● ½ onion, diced

- 1 cup quinoa ● 1 cup tomato puree

- 1 tablespoon fresh dill

- ½ bell pepper, chopped

- 1 cup of water ● 1 teaspoon salt

- 1 teaspoon cayenne pepper

- 1/3 cup green peas

- 1 teaspoon almond butter

Directions:

8. Toss butter in the instant pot and melt it on Saute mode.

9. Add carrot, onion, and bell pepper. Saute the ingredients for 10minutes. Mix p them from time to time.

10.   After this, add quinoa, green peas, cayenne pepper, salt,fresh dill, and water.

11.   Add tomato puree, mix up the soup and close the lid.

12.   Set Manual (high pressure) mode and cook soup for 3minutes.

13.   Then use quick pressure release.

14.   Mix up the cooked soup well before serving.

Nutrition value/serving: calories 313, fat 6.9, fiber 8.4, carbs 53.3, protein12.2

Main Dishes

31.   Asian Steamed Dumplings

Prep time: 15 minutes **Cooking time:** 16 minutes

Servings: 5

Ingredients:

- ¼ cup mushrooms, chopped

- ½ carrot, grated

- ½ onion, diced

- ½ teaspoon ground black pepper

- 1 teaspoon soy sauce

- 1 teaspoon fish sauce

- 1 teaspoon coconut oil

- 5 dumpling wrappers

- 1 cup water, for cooking

Directions:

15.	Preheat instant pot on saute mode and place coconut oilinside.

16.	Melt it and add grated carrot, diced onion, and choppedmushrooms.

17.	Add soy sauce and fish sauce.

18.	Mix up vegetables well and cook them for 10 minuteson saute mode.

19.	When the time is over, stir the ingredients with the helpof the wooden spatula.

20.	Transfer the mixture in the mixing bowl, if it is cooked.Keep cooking for 2-3 minutes more if it wasn't ready yet.

21.	Then prepare dumpling wrappers.

22.	Brush the edges of the wrappers

with water and place the mushroom filling in the center.

23. Wrap the wrappers to make the dumpling shape.

24. Clean instant pot.

25. Pour water inside the instant pot and insert steamer rack.

26. Place dumplings on the steamer rack.

27. Set Steam mode and close the lid.

28. Cook the dumplings for 6 minutes. Make a natural pressure release.

Nutrition value/serving: calories 217, fat 1.4, fiber 2.5, carbs 45, protein 6.4

32.   Portobello Roast

Prep time: 25 minutes **Cooking time:** 30 minutes

Servings: 2

Ingredients:

- 2 Portobello mushrooms

- 1 carrot, chopped

- 1 potato, chopped

- ½ white onion, chopped

- 1 garlic clove, diced

- ½ teaspoon thyme

- ½ teaspoon rosemary

- 1 tablespoon mustard

- ½ cup of water

- 1 teaspoon tomato paste

- 1 teaspoon salt

- 1 teaspoon ground black pepper

- 1 tablespoon coconut oil

Directions:

16. Wash and trim the mushrooms.

17. Then rub them with salt and ground black peppergenerously.

18. Slice the mushrooms and transfer in the instant pot. Addcoconut oil.

19. Set saute mode and cook the vegetables for 3-5 minutes. Stir them from time to time.

20. Then sprinkle mushrooms with thyme and rosemary.

21. Add chopped potato, carrot, and diced onion.

22.   Add tomato paste, mustard, garlic, and water.

23.   Carefully mix up the mixture. Close and seal the lid.

24.   Set Manual mode (high pressure) and cook themushroom roast for 25 minutes.

25.   Then allow natural pressure release for 20 minutes.

26.   Transfer the cooked roast in the serving bowls and topwith the gravy.

Nutrition value/serving: calories 203, fat 8.6, fiber 5.7, carbs 27.4, protein

7

33.   Posole

Prep time: 35 minutes **Cooking time:** 8 minutes

Servings: 4

Ingredients:

- 2 cups hominy

- 1 cup red chili puree

- ½ red onion, sliced

- 2 garlic cloves, peeled, chopped

- 1 cup jackfruit, canned

- 4 cups vegetable broth

- 1 teaspoon almond butter

Directions:

16.   Set Saute mode and preheat

instant pot.

17.   Toss almond butter and melt it.

18.   After this, add sliced onion, chopped garlic, and redchili puree.

19.   Cook the mixture for 4 minutes. Stir it carefully.

20.   Add jackfruit and cook it for 3 minutes more.

21.   With the help of the hand masher, mash the mixturewell.

22.   Add vegetable broth; close and seal the lid.

23.   Cook the meal on Manual mode for 10 minutes. Then allow natural pressure release for 15 minutes.

24.   Open the lid, add hominy. Set Manual mode and cook the meal for 1 minute

more.

25.   Then allow natural pressure release for 20 minutes.

26.   Open the lid and mix up the meal carefully.

Nutrition value/serving: calories 189, fat 4.5, fiber 3.4, carbs 29.1, protein

7.8

34.   Lentil Gumbo

Prep time: 10 minutes **Cooking time:** 23 minutes

Servings: 4

Ingredients:

- ½ tablespoon garlic, diced

- ½ tablespoon coconut oil

- 1 bell pepper, chopped

- 1 celery stalk, chopped

- ½ teaspoon thyme

- 1.2 teaspoon coriander

- 1 teaspoon Cajun spices

- ½ teaspoon white pepper

- ½ cup lentils

- 1 ½ cup water

- ½ cup okra, chopped

- ½ cup tomatoes, diced, canned

- 1 teaspoon lemon juice

- 4 oz cauliflower, chopped

- 1 teaspoon salt

Directions:

10. Preheat instant pot on Saute mode and toss coconut oilinside.

11. Melt it and add bell pepper, garlic, celery stalk, thyme, coriander, and Cajun spices.

12. Mix up the mixture and cook for 10 minutes.

13. Then add all the remaining ingredients except salt.

14. Close and seal the lid.

15.   Set Manual mode (high pressure) and cook gumbo for13 minutes.

16.   Then make quick pressure release.

17.   Open the lid, add salt and mix up the meal well.

Nutrition value/serving: calories 129, fat 2.2, fiber 9.3, carbs 20.7, protein 7.7

35.   Chana Masala with Spinach

Prep time: 15 minutes **Cooking time:** 7 minutes

Servings: 5

Ingredients:

- 2 cups chickpeas, canned

- 6 cups spinach, chopped

- 2 oz tomato, chopped

- 1 tablespoon olive oil

- 1 white onion, diced

- 1 teaspoon cumin

- 1 teaspoon red chili powder

- 1 teaspoon turmeric

- 1 teaspoon paprika

- 1 teaspoon garam masala

- 1 tablespoon lime juice

- ½ teaspoon Pink salt

Directions:

16.   Put olive oil and diced onion in the instant pot.

17.   Set Saute mode and cook the ingredients for 4 minutes.

18.   Then make a quick stir and add chopped tomatoes, cumin, red chili powder, turmeric, paprika, garam masala, and Pinksalt.

19.   Add lime juice and mix the mixture up.

20.   Add chickpeas, mix up.

21.   Close and seal the lid.

22.   Set Manual mode (high pressure) and cook the meal for3 minutes.

23.   Make a quick pressure release.

24.   Open the lid and add spinach. Stir it carefully and closethe lid.

25.   Let the meal rest for 10 minutes before serving.

Nutrition value/serving: calories 341, fat 8.1, fiber 15.8, carbs 53.5, protein 17.1

Snacks and Appetizers

36.   Tempeh Potato Wraps

Prep: 10 minutes**Cooking:** 3 hours**Servings:** 6

Ingredients:

- 1 potato, peeled, chopped ● 8 oz tempeh, chopped ● 1 teaspoon brown sugar

- 1 tablespoon apple cider vinegar

- 1 tablespoon of liquid smoked

- 2 tablespoons tamari

- ½ teaspoon ground black pepper

- 1 tablespoon coconut oil

- 1 cup of water ● 6 corn tortillas

Directions:

12.   Place tempeh and chopped potato

in the instant pot.

13.   Add brown sugar, apple cider vinegar, liquid smoke, tamari, ground black pepper, coconut oil, and water.

14.   Close the lid and set slow cook mode.

15.   Cook the mixture for 3 hours.

16.   Then open the lid, mix up the ingredients.

17.   Fill the tortillas with cooked tempeh mixture and wrapthem.

Nutrition value/serving: calories 173, fat 7.1, fiber 2.2, carbs 20.2, protein 9.6

37. Vegan Nuggets

Prep: 10 minutes **Cooking:** 6 minutes**Servings:** 8

Ingredients:

- ½ cup panko bread crumbs

- 1 tablespoon turmeric ● 4 oz rolled oats

- 1 onion, diced ● 1 tablespoon olive oil

- ½ teaspoon ground black pepper

- 1 teaspoon salt

- 1 tablespoon coconut milk

- 1 cup chickpeas, canned

- 1 tablespoon tomato sauce

- ½ cup water for cooking

Directions:

13. Preheat instant pot on Saute mode.

14.   When it is hot, add olive oil and diced onion.

15.   Cook it for 3-4 minutes, stir from time to time.

16.   When the onion is soft, transfer it in the food processor.

17.   Add rolled oats, ground black pepper, salt, coconutmilk, canned chickpeas, and tomato sauce.

18.   Blend the mixture until smooth.

19.   In the separated bowl, mix up together turmeric andpanko bread crumbs.

20.   Make the medium size nuggets from the chickpeamixture.

21.   Then coat nuggets in the panko

bread mixture.

22.   Pour water in the instant pot and insert rack.

23.   Place instant pot pan on the rack and put nuggets inside

it.

24.   Close and seal the lid.

25.   Set manual mode (high pressure) and cook "nuggets"for 3 minutes.

26.   Then use quick pressure release.

27.   Chill the cooked snack till the room temperature.

Nutrition value/serving: calories 200, fat 5.1, fiber 6.7, carbs 31.7, protein 7.9

38.   Crunchwrap Supreme

Prep time: 15 minutes **Cooking time:** 10 minute

Servings: 4

Ingredients:

- 5 oz tofu, chopped

- 1 tablespoon olive oil

- 1 teaspoon taco seasoning

- 1 tablespoon salsa sauce

- 2 tablespoons queso sauce

- 4 burrito size tortillas

- 1/3 cup tortilla chips

- ½ cup black beans, canned

- 1 avocado, peeled, cored

- 1 tomato, chopped

- 1 teaspoon coconut oil

Directions:

18.   Pour olive oil in the instant pot and preheat it on Sautemode.

19.   Add chopped tofu and sprinkle it with taco seasoning.

20.   Cook it on saute mode for 2 minutes. Stir it.

21.   Then mash the avocado.

22.   Spread the burrito tortillas with mashed avocado.

23.   After this, add salsa sauce, cooked tofu, choppedtomatoes, and black beans.

24.   Repeat the same steps with all burrito tortillas.

25.   Place tortilla chips on the top of

black beans and wrapburrito tortillas.

26.   Toss coconut oil in the instant pot, melt it on Saute mode and add wrapped burrito tortillas.

27.   Cook them for 3 minutes from each side.

Nutrition value/serving: calories 518, fat 26.1, fiber 9.6, carbs 58.4,

protein 14.4

39. Spring Rolls

Prep time: 15 minutes **Cooking time:** 4 minutes

Servings: 6

Ingredients:

- ¼ cup red cabbage, shredded

- 2 oz fresh parsley, chopped

- 1 cup mushrooms, chopped

- 1 carrot, cut into wedges

- 1 tablespoon fish sauce

- 1 teaspoon paprika

- 1 tablespoon lemon juice

- ¼ teaspoon lime zest

- ½ teaspoon chili flakes

- 6 spring roll wraps

- 1 cup water, for cooking

Directions:

13.   In the mixing bowl, mix up together shredded red cabbage, fresh parsley, chopped mushrooms, carrot, fish sauce, paprika, lemon juice, lime zest, and chili flakes.

14.   Fill the spring roll wraps with cabbage mixture. Wrapthe spring roll wraps.

15.   Pour water in the instant pot, insert steamer rack inside.

16.   Place prepared spring rolls on the steamer rack.

17.   Close and seal the lid.

18.   Set Manual mode (high pressure) and cook the meal for4 minutes.

19.   Then allow natural pressure

release for 5 minutes.

Nutrition value/serving: calories 22, fat 0.2, fiber 1.9, carbs 4.5, protein 2

40.　Delicious Lettuce Wraps

Prep: 10 minutes **Cooking:** 4 minutes**Servings:** 4

Ingredients:

- 4 lettuce leaves ● 3 oz vegan Parmesan, grated

- 1 cucumber, chopped

- 1 tablespoon chives, chopped

- 8 oz tempeh, chopped

- 1 tablespoon Italian seasoning

- 3 tablespoons tomato sauce

- ¼ cup tomato juice ● 1 teaspoon brown sugar

- 1/3 cup turnip, chopped

Directions:

11.　　In the instant pot, combine together chopped tempeh, Italian seasoning, tomato sauce, tomato juice, brown sugar, and turnip.

12.   Mix up the mixture, close and seal the instant pot lid.

13.   Cook it on Manual for 4 minutes; use quick pressurerelease.

14.   After this, mix up together grated Parmesan choppedcucumber, and chives.

15.   Place the mixture on the lettuce leaves.

16.   Chill the tempeh mixture till the room temperature.

17.   Transfer it over the vegetables and wrap the lettuceleaves.

Nutrition value/serving: calories 209, fat 7.3, fiber 0.9, carbs 15.7, protein20.1

Sauces and Fillings

41.   Vegan French Sauce

Prep time: 10 minutes **Cooking time:** 6 minutes

Servings: 5

Ingredients:

- 1 cup mushrooms, chopped • ½ cup vegetable stock • 1 teaspoon salt • 4 oz firm tofu

- 1 tablespoon olive oil

- 1 teaspoon ground black pepper

- 1 tablespoon almond yogurt

- 1 teaspoon potato starch

Directions:

18.   Pour vegetable stock in the instant pot.

19.   Add mushrooms, salt, tofu, olive oil, ground black pepper, almond yogurt, and close the lid.

20.   Cook the dip on manual mode (high pressure) for 6minutes.

21.   Then make quick pressure release.

22.   Open the lid and add potato starch.

23.   Blend the mixture with the help of the hand blender until smooth. The sauce is cooked.

Nutrition value/serving: calories 51, fat 4.3, fiber 0.5, carbs 2.4, protein 2.4

42.   Pumpkin Butter

Prep time: 5 minutes **Cooking time:** 3 minutes

Servings: 4

Ingredients:

- ½ cup pumpkin puree

- 3 tablespoons orange juice

- 1 tablespoon sugar

- 1 tablespoon almond butter

- ¾ teaspoon salt

- 1 teaspoon pumpkin pie spices

Directions:

14.   Put pumpkin puree, orange juice, sugar, almond butter,and salt in the instant pot.

15.   Sprinkle the mixture with pumpkin pie spices and stirwell.

16.   Close and seal the lid.

17.   Cook the butter for 3 minutes on Manual mode (highpressure).

18.   Then make quick pressure release. Open the lid andtransfer the meal in the bowl.

19.   Chill it for 20-30 minutes before serving.

Nutrition value/serving: calories 53, fat 2.4, fiber 1.4, carbs 7.7, protein

1.3

43. Cranberry Sauce

Prep time: 10 minutes **Cooking time:** 2 minutes

Servings: 6

Ingredients:

- 8 oz cranberries

- 3 oz maple syrup

- 1 tablespoon lemon juice

- ¾ teaspoon dried oregano

Directions:

15.   Place cranberries, maple syrup, lemon juice, and dried oregano in the instant pot. Stir gently.

16.   Close and seal the lid.

17.   Cook the sauce on manual mode for 2 minutes. When the time is over, allow

natural pressure release for 5 minutes more.

18.   Stir the sauce gently before serving.

Nutrition value/serving: calories 59, fat 0.1, fiber 1.5, carbs 13.1, protein 0

44.   Spinach Dip

Prep: 10 minutes **Cooking:** 10 minutes**Servings:** 4

Ingredients:

- 1 teaspoon onion powder

- 2 cups spinach, chopped

- ½ cup artichoke hearts, canned, chopped

- 1 tablespoon olive oil

- 1 teaspoon ground black pepper

- 1 teaspoon salt

- ½ cup of coconut yogurt

- 1 teaspoon cornstarch

- 4 oz vegan Parmesan, grated

Directions:

15.   Preheat the instant pot on Saute mode.

16.   Then pour olive oil inside.

17.   Add chopped spinach and chopped artichoke hearts.

18.   Sprinkle the greens with ground black pepper and salt.Stir it well.

19.   Close the lid and cook on Saute mode for 5 minutes.

20.   After this, add coconut yogurt, onion powder, andcornstarch.

21.   Add grated Parmesan and mix up the mixture well.

22.   Cook it for 5 minutes more.

Nutrition value/serving: calories 150, fat 4.1, fiber 1.6, carbs 11.5, protein 13.3

45.   Red Kidney Beans Sauce

Prep time: 10 minutes **Cooking time:** 35 minutes

Servings: 4

Ingredients:

- ½ cup red kidney beans, soaked

- 2 cups of water

- 1 tablespoon tomato paste

- 1 bell pepper, chopped

- 1 teaspoon salt

- 1 teaspoon chili flakes

- ½ teaspoon white pepper

- 1 tablespoon corn flour

- ¼ cup fresh dill, chopped

Directions:

17.   In the instant pot, combine

together red kidney beans, water, tomato paste, chopped bell pepper, salt, chili flakes, white pepper, and dill.

18.   Mix up the mixture well.

19.   Close and seal the instant pot lid.

20.   Set manual mode and cook the ingredients for 30minutes.

21.   Then use quick pressure release and open the lid.

22.   Add corn flour and mix up the sauce well.

23.   Close the lid.

24.   Saute the sauce for 5 minutes on Saute mode.

25.   Then stir it well and let chill till

the room temperature.

Nutrition value/serving: calories 105, fat 0.6, fiber

4.7, carbs 20.4, protein

6.4

Desserts

46. Cranberry Cake

Prep time: 15 minutes **Cooking time:** 30 minutes

Servings: 6

Ingredients:

- 8 oz wheat flour

- ¼ teaspoon ground cinnamon

- ½ teaspoon ground cardamom

- ½ teaspoon baking powder

- ½ cup of coconut milk

- ½ cup of sugar

- 4 oz cranberries, chopped

- Cooking spray

- 1 cup water, for cooking

Directions:

28. In the mixing bowl mix up together wheat flour, ground cinnamon, cardamom, baking powder, coconut milk, and sugar.

29. When the mixture is homogenous, add chopped cranberries and stir it carefully.

30. Spray the bundt pan with the cooking spray from inside and transfer the mixed dough.

31. Flatten it gently with the help of the spatula. Cover the pan with the parchment or foil. Secure the edges.

32. Pour water in the instant pot.

Insert bundt pan and closethe lid.

33.   Set Manual mode (high pressure) and cook cake for 30 minutes. Allow natural pressure release for 20 minutes.

34.   When the cake is cooked, discard the foil/[archment from it and chill it till the room temperature. Slice it.

Nutrition value/serving: calories 258, fat 5.2, fiber 2.3, carbs 48.8, protein

4.4

47.   Apple Crumble

Prep time: 20 minutes **Cooking time:** 14 minutes

Servings: 4

Ingredients:

- ¼ cup coconut flakes

- 1 cup rolled oats

- ¼ cup wheat flour

- 3 tablespoons cashew butter

- 1 teaspoon vanilla extract

- 1 cup apples, chopped

- 1 tablespoon brown sugar

- 1 tablespoon maple syrup

- ¾ cup of soy milk

- Cooking spray

- ½ cup of water

Directions:

28.   In the mixing bowl combine together coconut flakes, rolled oats, wheat flour, cashew butter, vanilla extract, brown sugar, and soy milk.

29.   Add maple syrup and stir it until homogenous.

30.   Spray the pan with the cooking spray.

31.   Make the crumble: place 1 tablespoon of the coconutflake dough in the pan, flatten it well to make the layer, then add chopped apples, after this repeat the steps till you use all the ingredients.

32.   Cover the pan with the foil.

33.   Pour water in the instant pot and insert pan.

34.   Close and seal the lid.

35.   Cook the crumble on High-pressure mode for 14 minutes. Then use quick pressure release.

36.   Discard the foil from the crumble and let it chill for 10minutes.

Nutrition value/serving: calories 273, fat 9.9, fiber 4.6, carbs 40.2, protein

7.4

48. Gajar Halwa

Prep time: 10 minutes **Cooking time:** 15 minutes

Servings: 2

Ingredients:

- 2 teaspoons coconut oil

- 1 oz cashew, chopped

- ½ oz raisins

- 1 ½ cup carrot, grated

- 4 tablespoons coconut milk

- ¾ teaspoon cardamom powder

- ¾ teaspoon ground cinnamon

- 1 tablespoon semolina

- Cooking spray

Directions:

23.   Preheat instant pot well on Saute

mode.

24.   Then add chopped cashews and raisins. Cook them onSaute mode for 3 minutes. Stit from time to time.

25.   After this, add grated carrot, cardamom powder, and ground cinnamon. Add coconut milk.

26.   Mix up the ingredients well.

27.   Close the lid and cook the mixture on Manual mode for 2 minutes. Then make a quick pressure release and open the lid.

28.   Add all the remaining ingredients and stir well.

29.   Saute the meal for 10 minutes. Stir it from time to time.

30.   Then chill the cooked halwa gently and transfer into thebowl.

Nutrition value/serving: calories 268, fat 18.4, fiber 4.3, carbs 25, protein 4.5

49.   Chocolate Cake

Prep time: 40 minutes **Cooking time:** 40 minutes

Servings: 6

Ingredients:

- 1 cup wheat flour

- 2 tablespoons cocoa powder

- 1 teaspoon vanilla extract

- 1 teaspoon baking powder

- 1 teaspoon apple cider vinegar

- ½ cup cashew milk • 1 cup coconut cream

- 2 tablespoons dark chocolate, melted

- Cooking spray

- 1 cup water for cooking

Diections:

26.   In the mixing bowl, mix up

together all dry ingredients.

27.   Then add apple cider vinegar,

vanilla extract, andcashew milk.

28.   Mix up the chocolate batter until

homogenous.

29.   Spray the springform pan with

the cooking spray and pour chocolate batter

inside.

30.   Pour water in the instant pot.

31.   Cover the pan with foil and

secure edges. Place it in theinstant pot.

32.   Close and seal the instant pot lid.

33.   Cook the cake on High-pressure

mode (manual mode)for 40 minutes.

34.   Then allow natural pressure

release for 15 minutes.

35.   Meanwhile, whisk together melted chocolate andcoconut cream.

36.   Transfer the cake on the plate and chill it well.

37.   Cut it into 2 cake layers.

38.   Spread every cake layer with the coconut creammixture.

39.   Combine the cake layers in the cake.

40.   Place it in the fridge for 30 minutes then cut it intoservings.

Nutrition value/serving: calories 196, fat 11.2, fiber 2.1, carbs 21.8, protein 3.7

50.   Pumpkin Muffins

Prep time: 15 minutes **Cooking time:** 10 minutes

Servings: 4

Ingredients:

- 4 teaspoons pumpkin puree

- 4 tablespoons wheat flour

- 1 teaspoon baking powder

- 1 teaspoon apple cider vinegar

- 1 teaspoon ground cinnamon

- 1 tablespoon coconut oil

- 2 teaspoons sugar

- ½ cup water, for cooking

Directions:

23. In the mixing bowl, mix up together pumpkin puree, wheat flour, baking powder,

apple cider vinegar, ground cinnamon, and sugar.

24. Then add coconut oil and stir it until smooth. The muffin batter is cooked.

25. Pour water in the instant pot and set steamer rack.

26. Then fill ½ of every muffin mold with muffin batter and transfer them on the steamer rack.

27. Close and seal the lid.

28. Set Manual mode (high pressure) and cook muffins for 10minutes.

29. Then allow natural pressure release for 10 minutes more.

30. Open the lid and transfer the cooked

muffins on the servingplate.

Nutrition value/serving: calories 70, fat 3.5, fiber 0.7, carbs 9.4, protein 0.9

Conclusion

Presently, the world is divided into people who support veganism and those who are against the complete abandonment of animal products. Hope this book could dispel your stereotypes that vegetarian food is monotonous and not tasty. If you have already read some pages of the cookbook, you know that it includes hundreds of magnificent and very easy to cook recipes. It is possible to say that this vegan recipe guide can be a good gift to everyone who loves delicious food. These days veganism is a sought-after way of life. More often people refuse to consume all types of meat and dairy products and limit yourself with fruits, vegetables, and another produces. It is true that thanks to the vegan lifestyle you can improve your health and feel much better. Scientifically proved that total refusing from any type of meat and dairy products can help fight with Type

9 781802 891881